RECORDED VERSIONS GUITAR

AUTHENTIC TRANSCRIPTIONS
WITH NOTES AND TABLATURE

jeff beck truth

Music transcriptions by Aurelien Budynek, Ron Piccione and David Stocker

ISBN 978-1-4234-9442-3

HAL•LEONARD®
CORPORATION

7777 W. BLUEMOUND RD. P.O. BOX 13819 MILWAUKEE, WI 53213

Visit Hal Leonard Online at
www.halleonard.com

Shapes of Things

Words and Music by Paul Samwell-Smith, James McCarty and Keith Relf

help me to de - spise. Will time make men more

wise?

Here with -

*Hold bend while performing hammer-on/pull-off sequence.

in my lone-ly frame, _____ my eyes just hurt _____ my

brain. _____ Will time make men more

4

than to - day.

*Hypothetical fret locations.

**Using a guitar with Les Paul style electronics, set rhythm volume to 0 and
lead volume to 10. Strike the strings while the pickup selector is in the lead
position, then flip the switch in the rhythm indicated to simulate the re-attack.

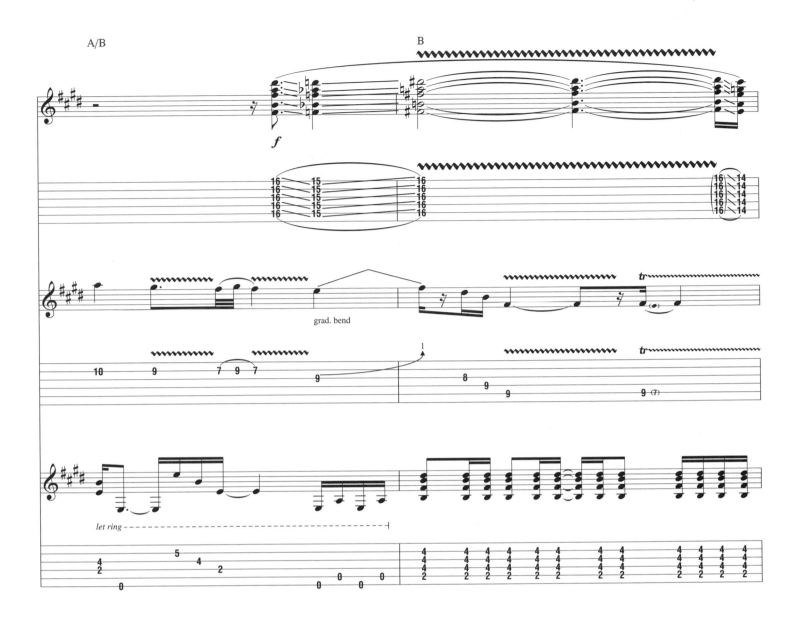

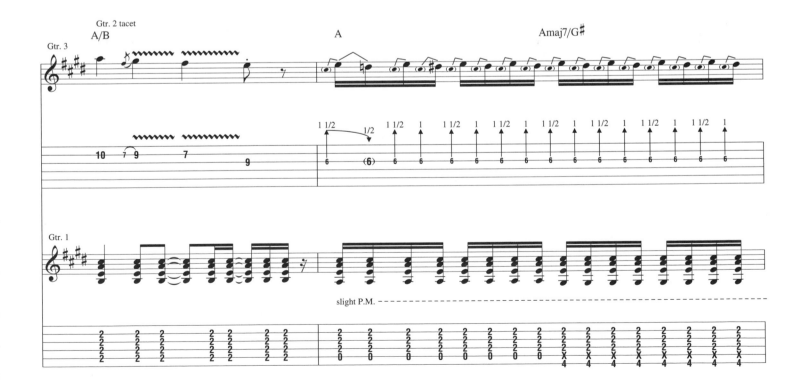

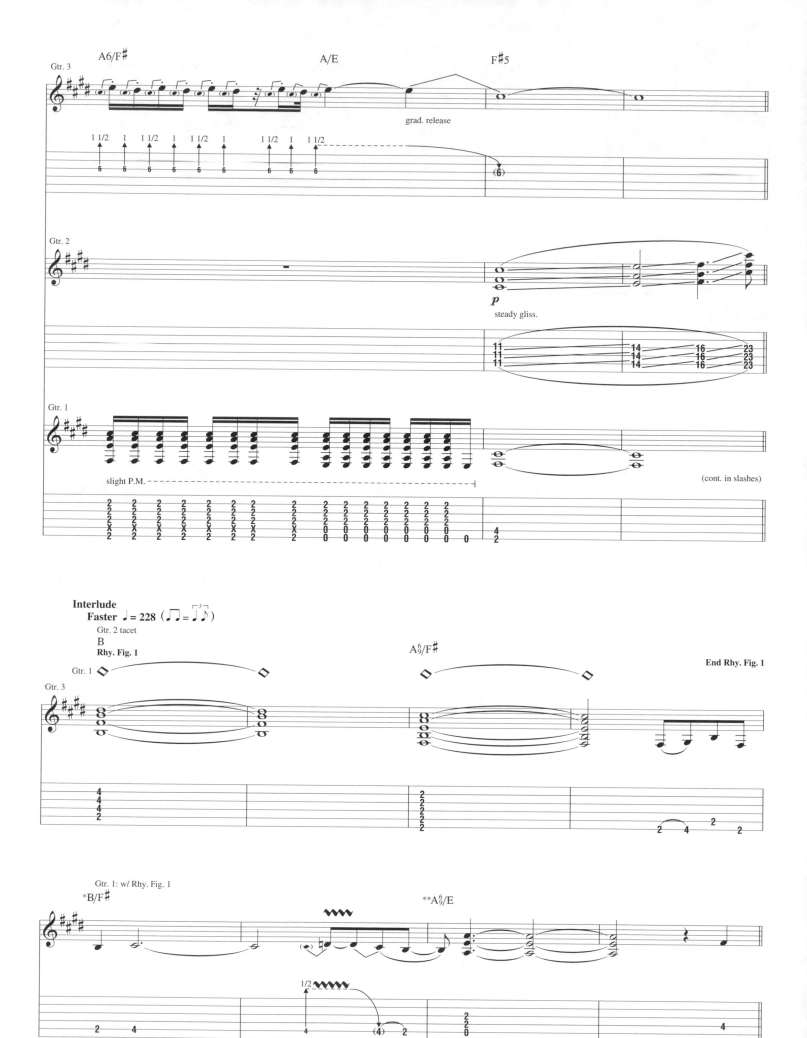

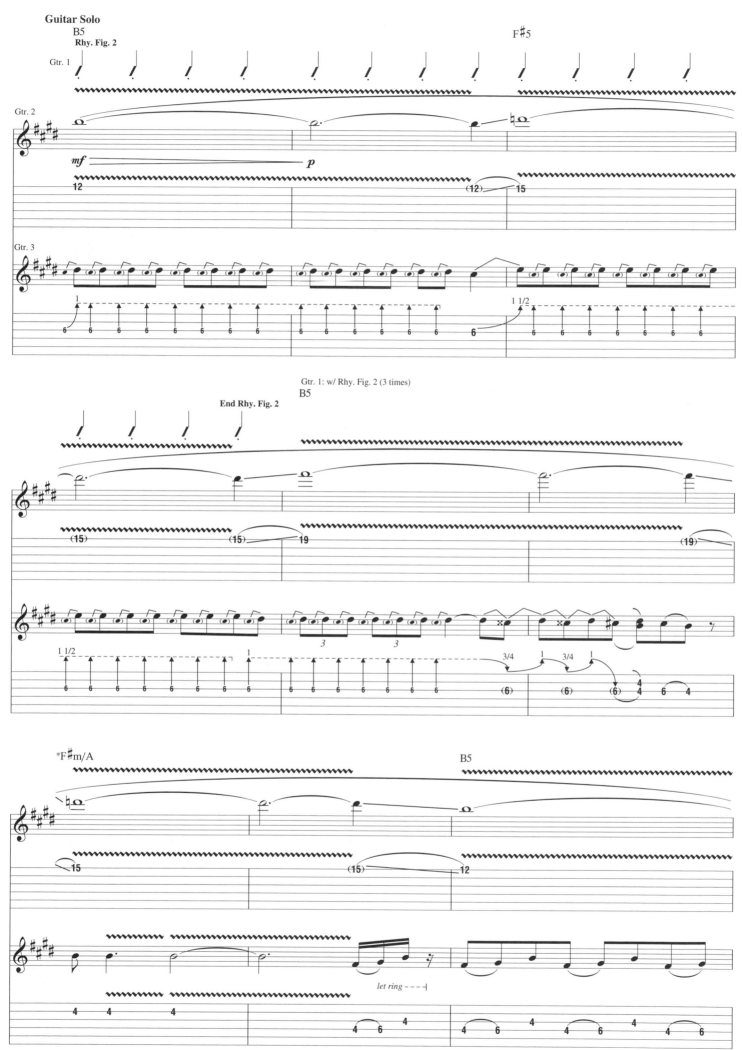

Guitar Solo

*Bass plays A.

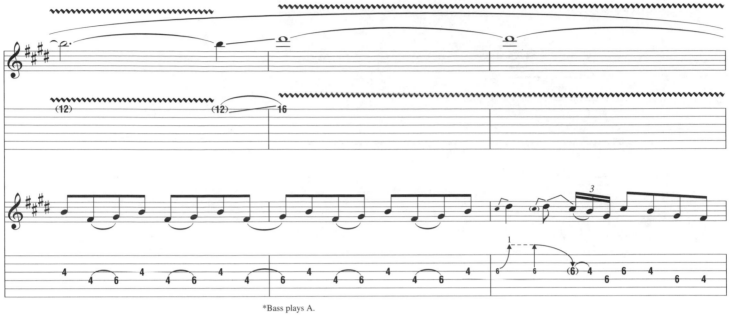

*F#m/A

*Bass plays A.

B5   F#5

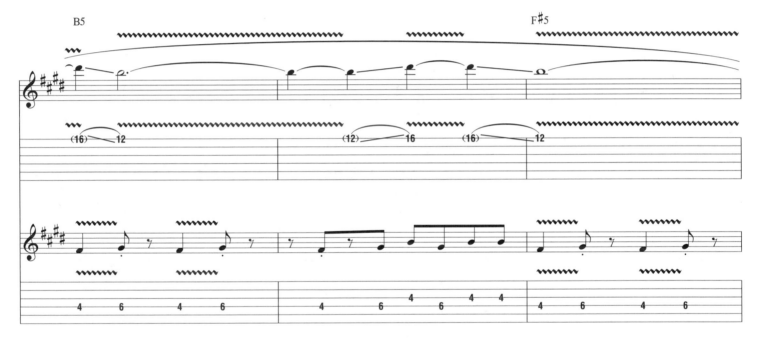

Gtr. 1: w/ Rhy. Fig. 1 (3 times)

B

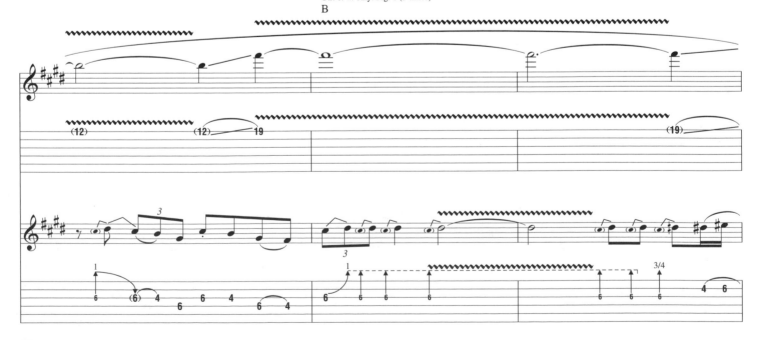

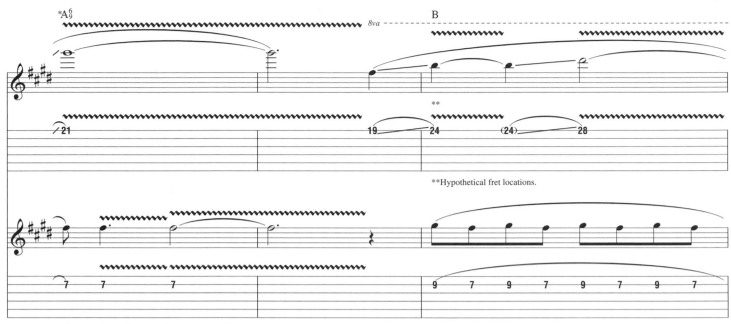

**Hypothetical fret locations.

*Chord symbols reflect overall harmony, next 10 meas.

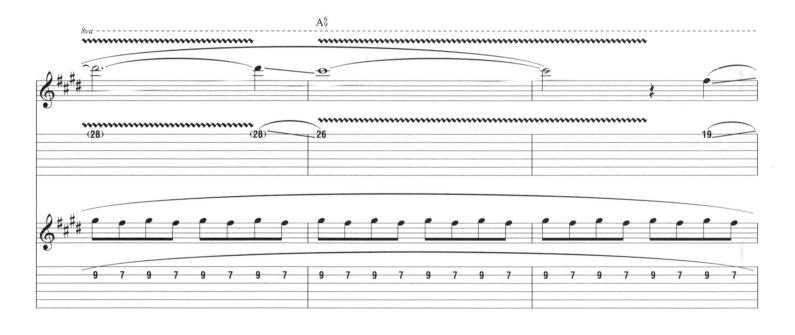

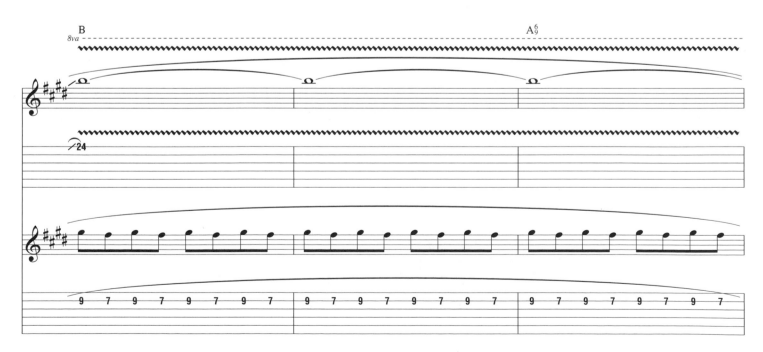

Outro

Gtr. 1 tacet

*Hypothetical fret locations.

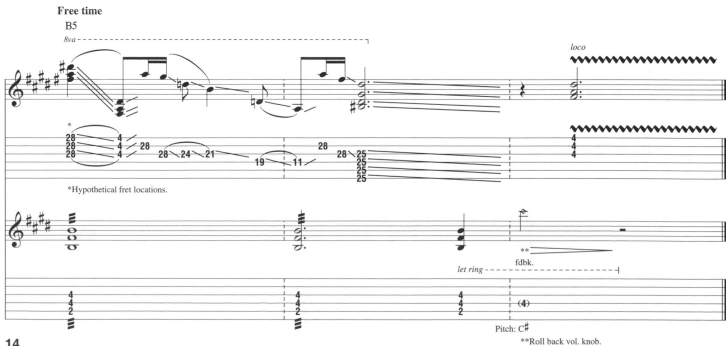

Pitch: C#

**Roll back vol. knob.

14

Let Me Love You

Words and Music by Rod Stewart and Jeff Beck

*Chord symbols reflect implied harmony.

(Rod Stewart) 1. O - va here. Let me love you, ba - by. You're driv-in' my poor heart cra - zy.

Let me love you, ba - by. You're

driv-in' my poor _____ heart cra - zy.

When I'm with you, wom - an, my whole life seems ___ so ha -

- zy.

2. Ah, _____ don't ___ you know ___ that

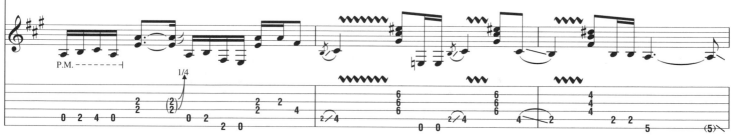

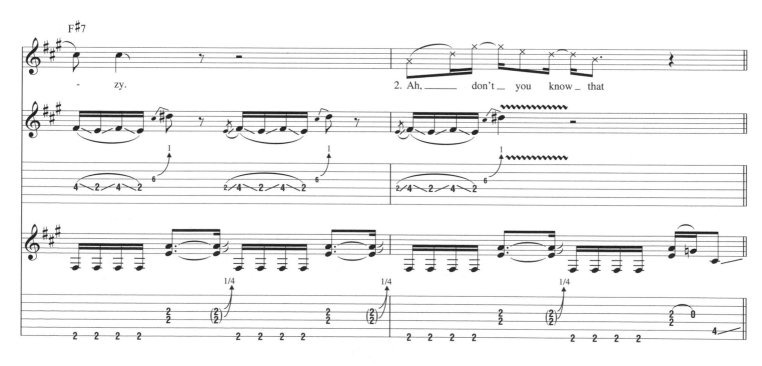

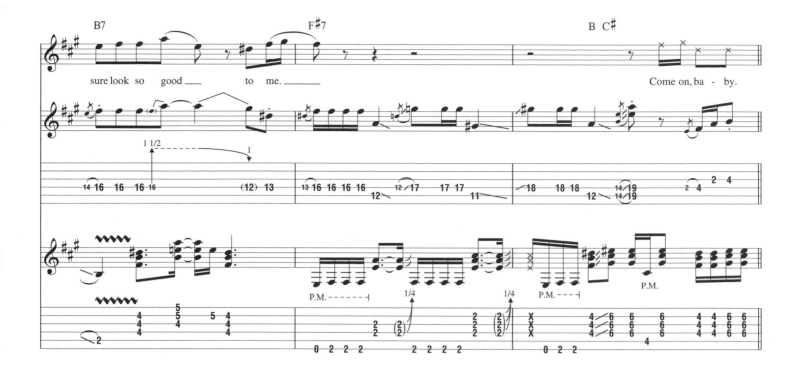

sure look so good _____ to me. _____ Come on, ba - by.

Guitar Solo

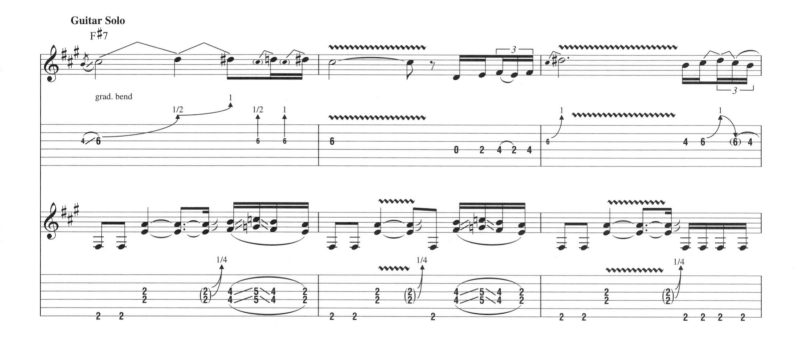

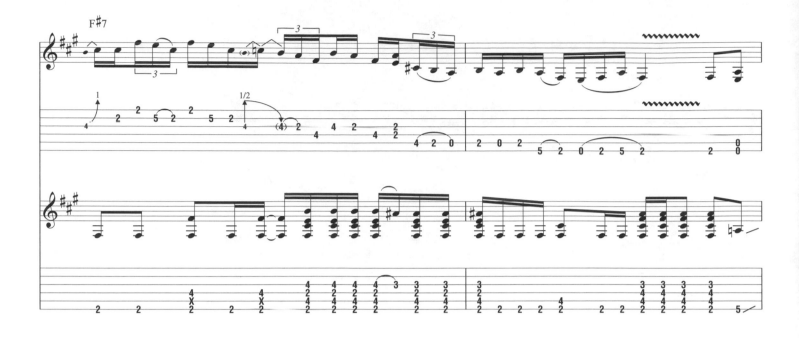

Yes, I ___ know. ___

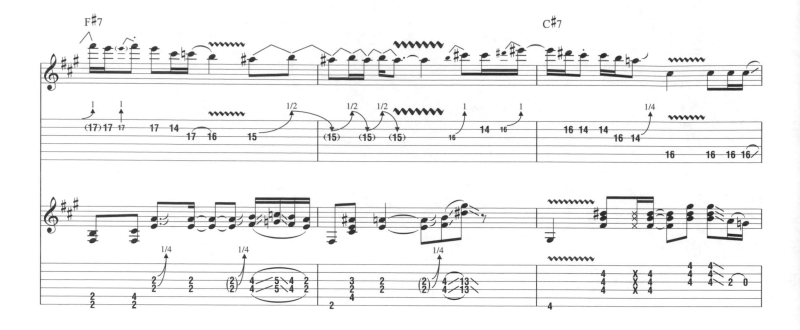

Verse

3. Ba - by, when __ you walk, __ you shake like a wil - low __ tree. __

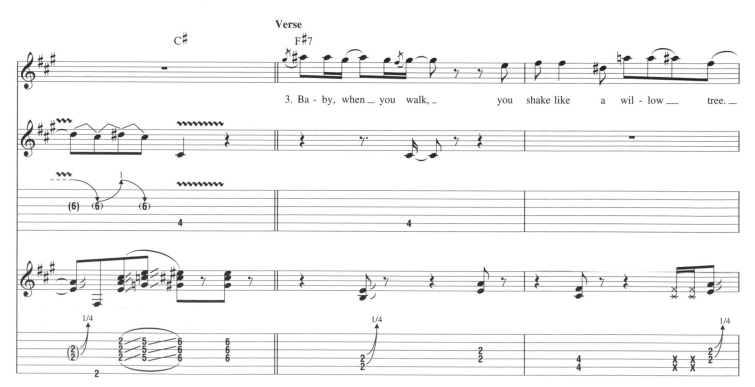

You ought - a know that by now.

Ba - by, when you walk, you shake like a wil - low tree.

And ooh, ee, ba - by, you sure look so good to me.

Outro

Eas - y with this one.

Let me love you, ba - by. ___

Love you, babe. ___ I know, I know, ___ I know.

w/ slide

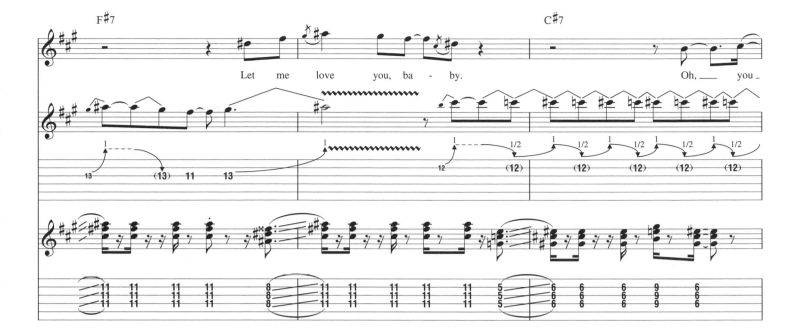

Let me love you, ba - by. Oh, ___ you ___

let me love you. ___ What ___ you got.

Let me love you, ba - by. Love ___

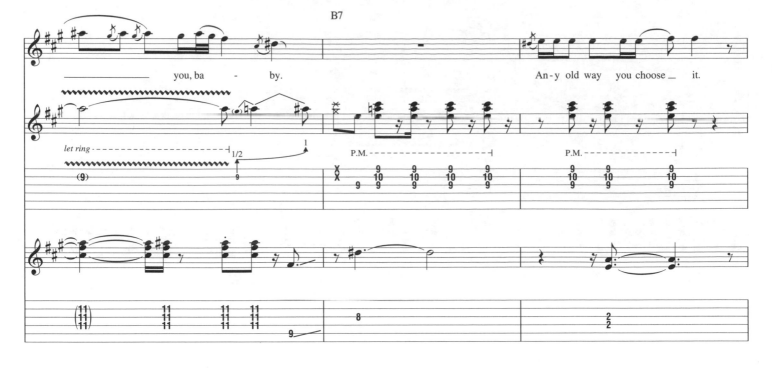

you, ba - by.   An-y old way you choose it.

I don't mind which time you call me.   Ah, ah,

yeah.   You're driv - in' my poor heart

cra - zy.   Let   me   love _____ you, ba - by.

Love _____ you, ba - by.

Ear - ly   in   the morn - in' time,   ah, _____

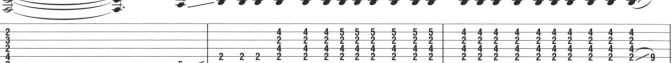

lat - er in __ the eve - nin'.   Let me

love   you, ba - by.   You're driv - in'   my poor   heart

cra - zy.

(Walk Me Out in The) Morning Dew

Words and Music by Bonnie Dobson and Tim Rose

*Chord symbols reflect overall harmony.

**Gtr. 1 (slight dist.); Gtr. 2 (dist.): w/ wah-wah & delay. Set vol. knob at 1/2 volume.
Composite arrangement

Rod Stewart: 1. Walk me out___ in the morn - in' ___ dew, my hon-ey.

Please _ walk me out _ in the morn - in' _ dew, some - time. _

Can't walk you out _ in no morn - in' dew, I'm sor - ry, I'm sor - ry.

*Decrease vol. knob to 1/4 volume.   **Increase vol. knob to 3/4 volume.   ***Vol. swell to full volume.

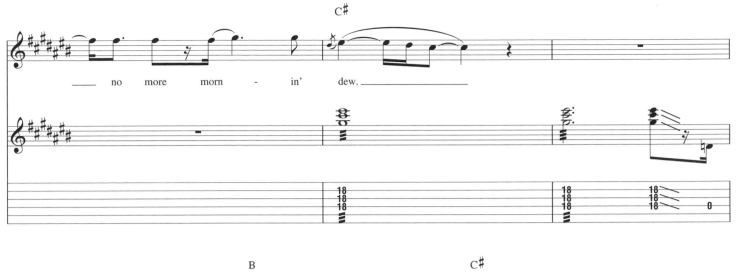

____ no more morn - in' dew. _____

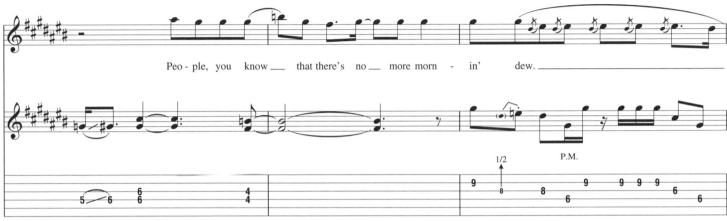

Peo - ple, you know ___ that there's no more morn - in' dew. _____

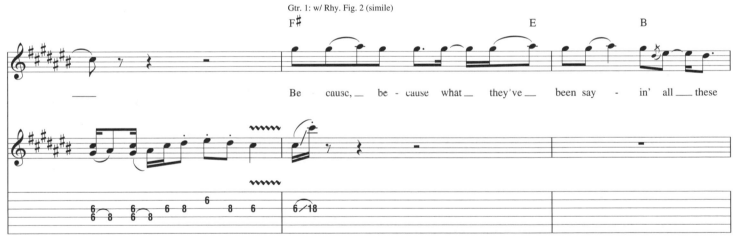

Gtr. 1: w/ Rhy. Fig. 2 (simile)

___ Be cause, ___ be - cause what ___ they've ___ been say - in' all ___ these

Gtr. 1: w/ Rhy. Fig. 3 (simile)

years has come true, and it had to hap - pen. You know _____

*Decrease vol. knob to 1/2 volume.

that, there's no more morn-in' dew, oo, oo.

You Shook Me

Words and Music by Willie Dixon and J.B. Lenoir

* Chord symbols reflect overall harmony.

long.   And the way that you

love me, ba - by, ___   you know what you do?   You mess up   my head _____ be - yond.

Take this.   2. You know you   love   me _____

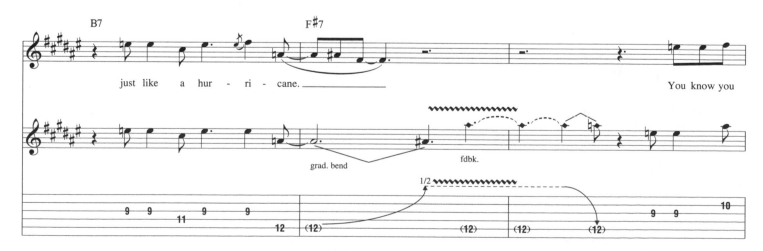

just like a hur - ri - cane. _____   You know you

love me _____ just like a hur - ri - cane, ____ ah.

And the way that you ____ love me, ba - by, you mess up my head ____ be - yond,

I'm so hap - py.

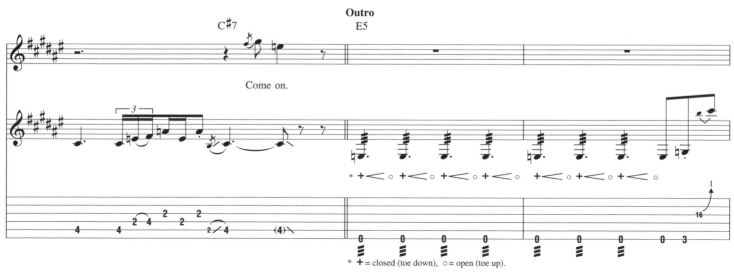

Come on.

* + = closed (toe down), o = open (toe up).

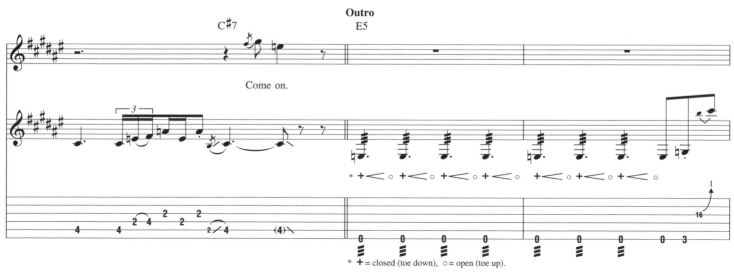

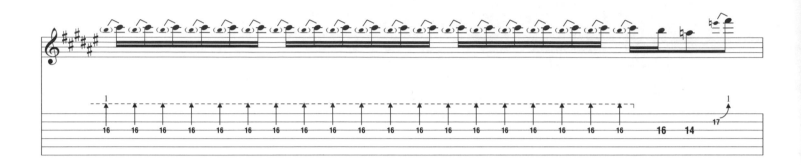

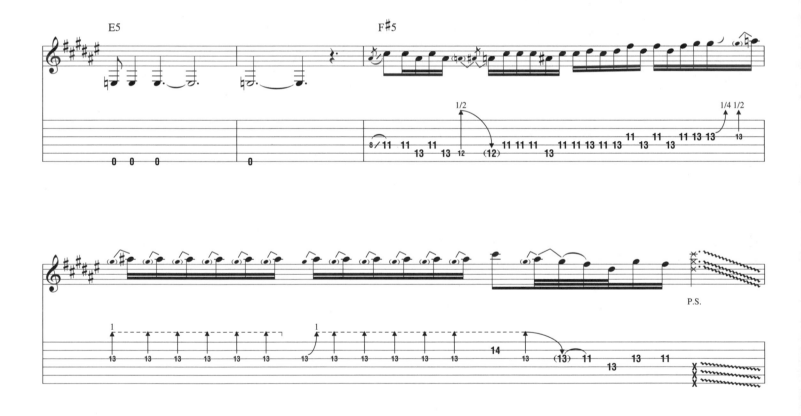

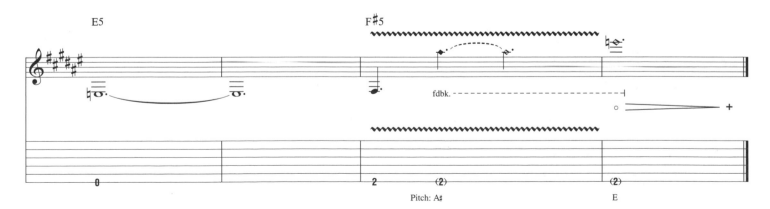

Ol' Man River

from SHOW BOAT

Lyrics by Oscar Hammerstein II
Music by Jerome Kern

*Not indicative of ensemble harmony.   **Chord symbols reflect overall harmony.

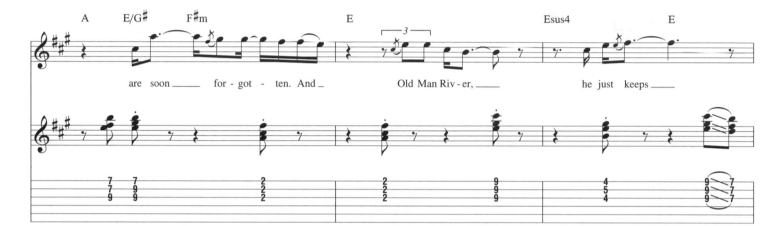

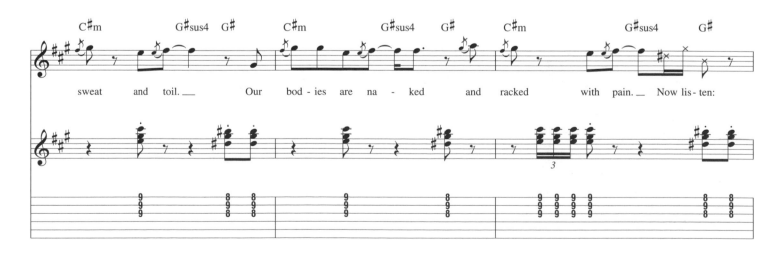

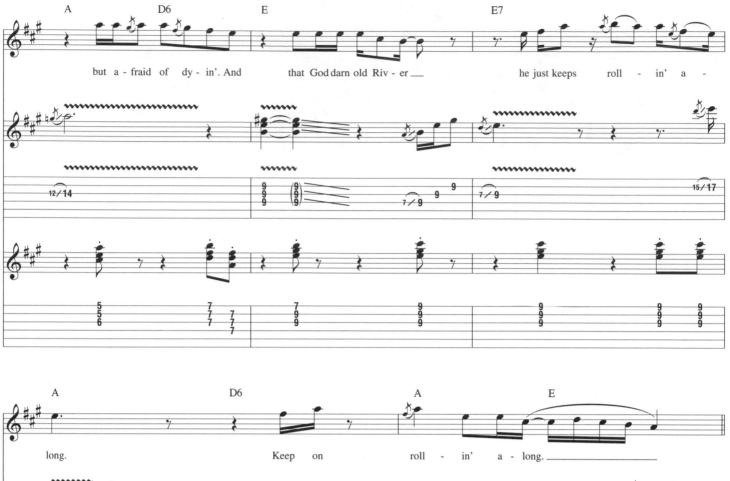

but a-fraid of dy-in'. And that God darn old Riv-er ___ he just keeps roll-in' a -

long. Keep on roll-in' a-long. _____

Interlude

Gtr. 2 tacet

*N.C.

(Organ, Bass & Drums, next 6 meas.)

Gtr. 1

*Not indicative of ensemble harmony.

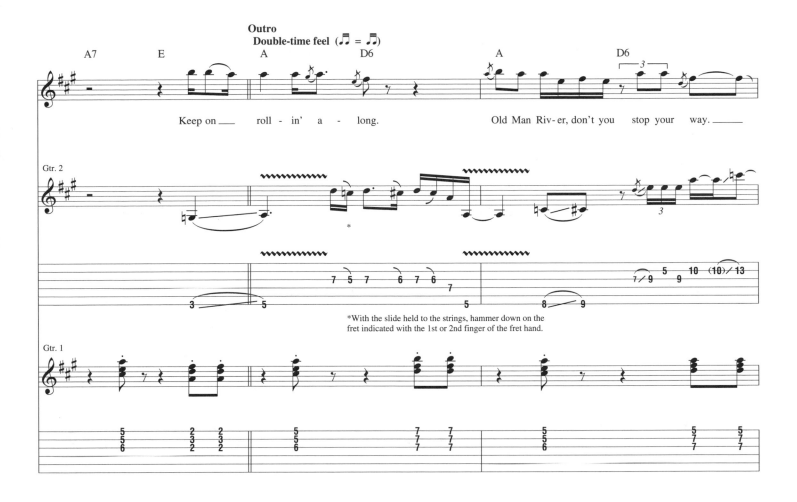

*With the slide held to the strings, hammer down on the
fret indicated with the 1st or 2nd finger of the fret hand.

Greensleeves

Arrangement by Rod Stewart and Jeff Beck

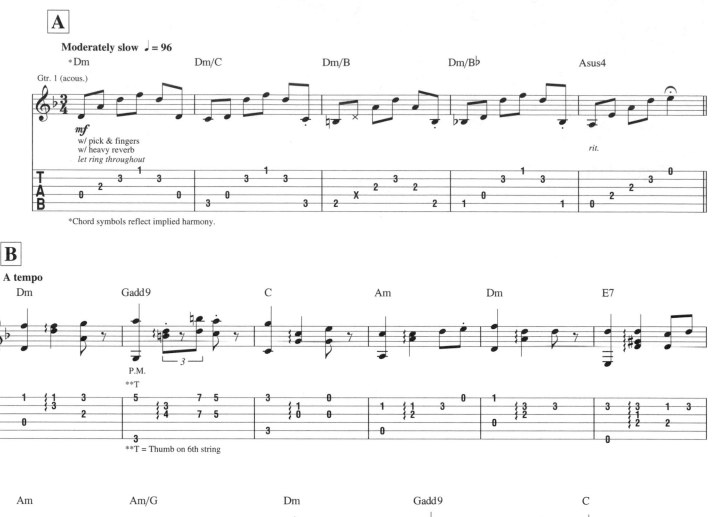

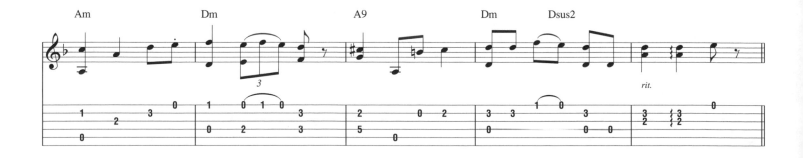

Slightly faster ♩ = 102

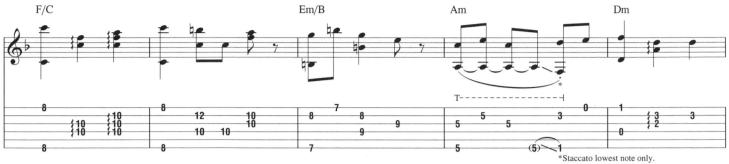

*Staccato lowest note only.

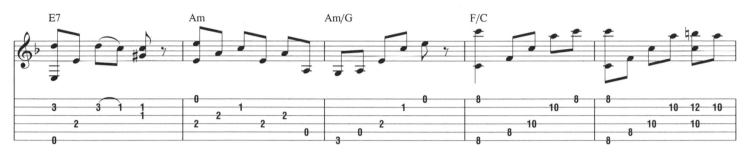

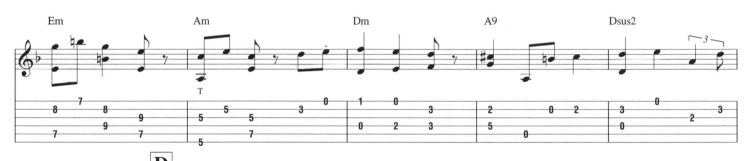

D

Slower ♩ = 87

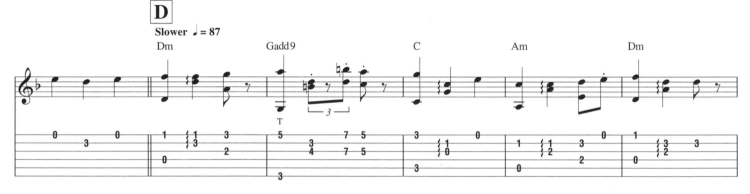

Free time

Rock My Plimsoul

Words and Music by Rod Stewart and Jeff Beck

*Chord symbols reflect overall harmony.

*Played as even eighth-notes.

Lis - ten.   1. You can rock __

__ me,   rock   me   all __ night __ long. __

Verse

**Gtrs. 1 & 2

**Composite arrangement

Keep on   rock - in' me, ba - by, _____   rock   me   all

night   long.   'Cause, you know what? When   you   rock   me

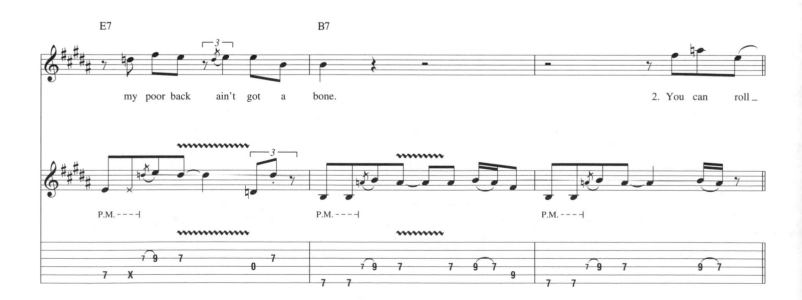

my poor back   ain't got a   bone.   2. You can   roll _

Guitar Solo

*Played as even eighth-notes.

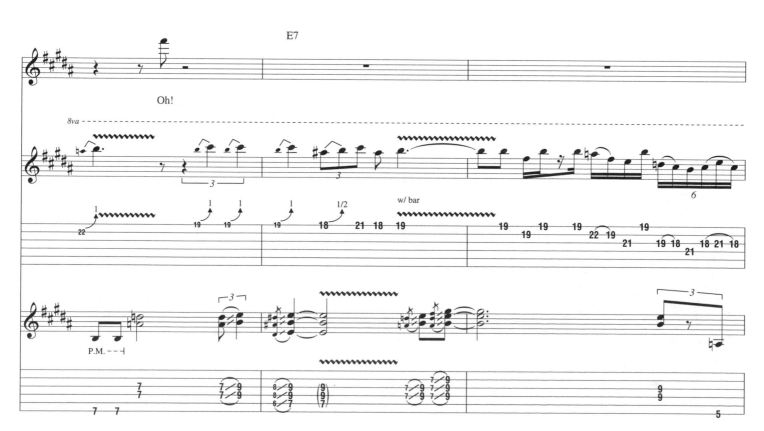

Oh!

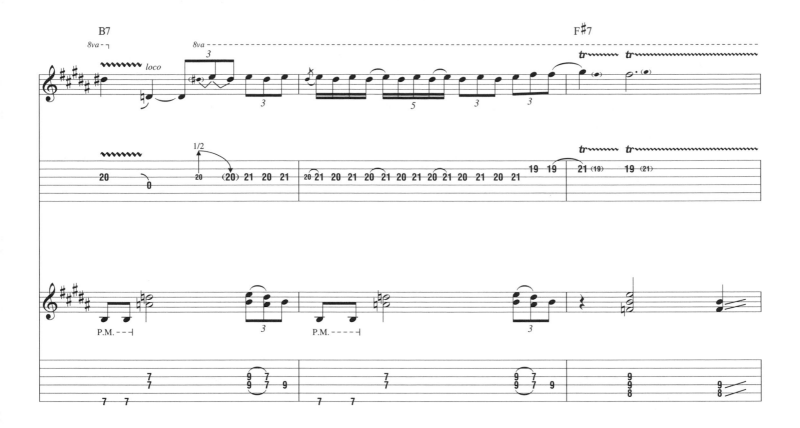

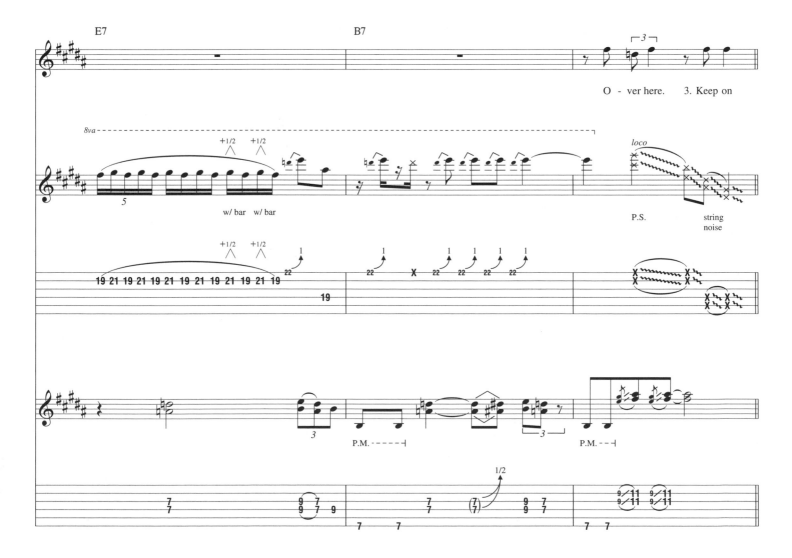

O - ver here.   3. Keep on

all night long.   'Cause you know what? When you shake, rat-tle and roll___

*Sung as even eighth-notes.

me,   my old back ain't got a bone.   So when you do it, keep on

Bridge

roll - in' me, ba - by, roll - in' me, babe. _____ An-

- y old way ___ you choose ___ it, keep on roll - in' me.

Hah, hah, keep roll - in' me, hon-ey, 'til ___ my old back ain't got a

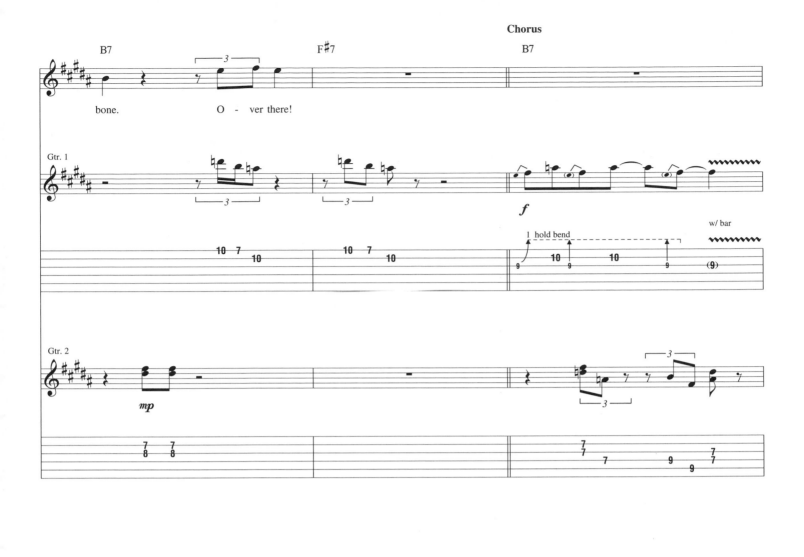

keep on ___ rock - in' me all night long.   You can ___ rock   me, ba - by, yeah,   yeah. ___

Free time

*Hypothetical fret location.

Beck's Bolero

By Jimmy Page

*Two gtrs. (elec. w/ clean tone & 12-str. acous.) arr. for one.

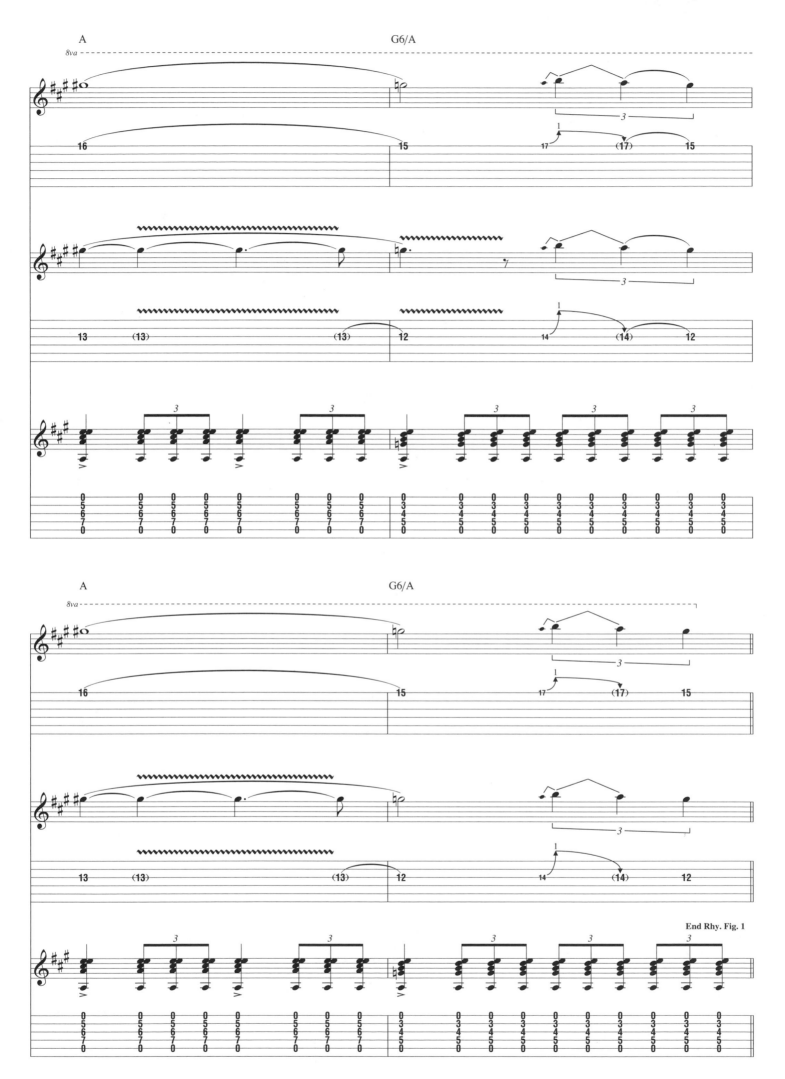

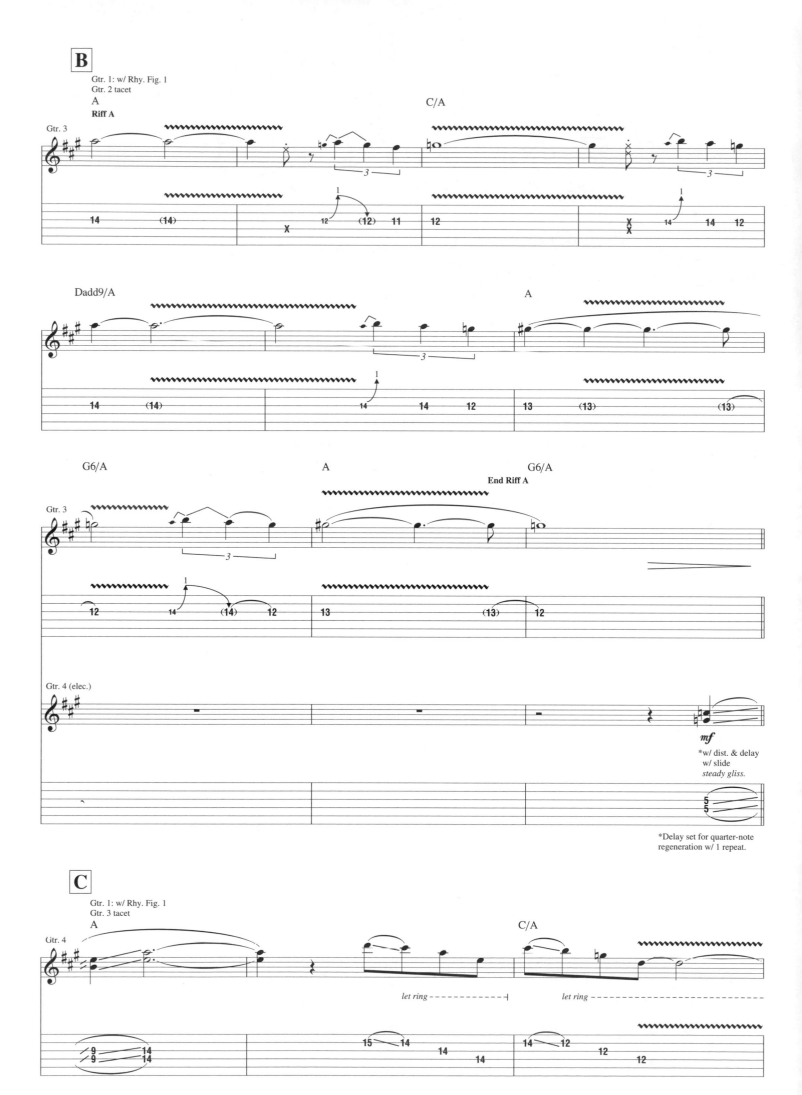

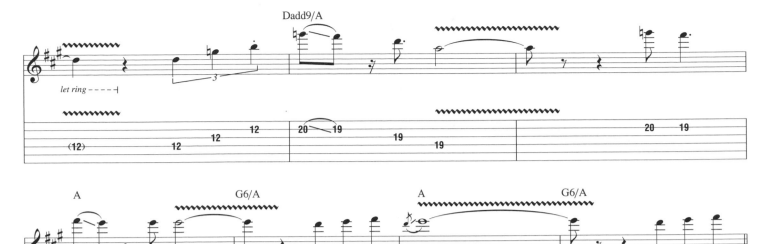

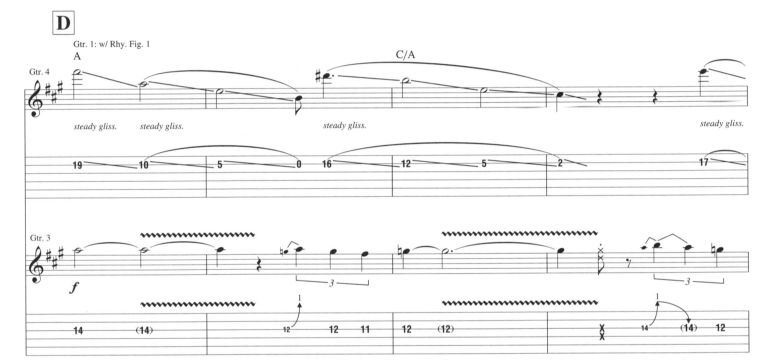

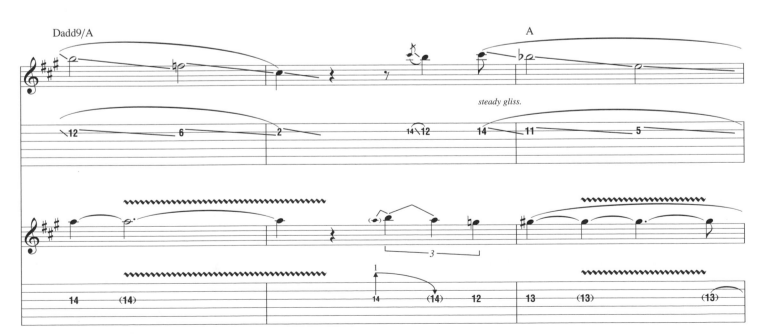

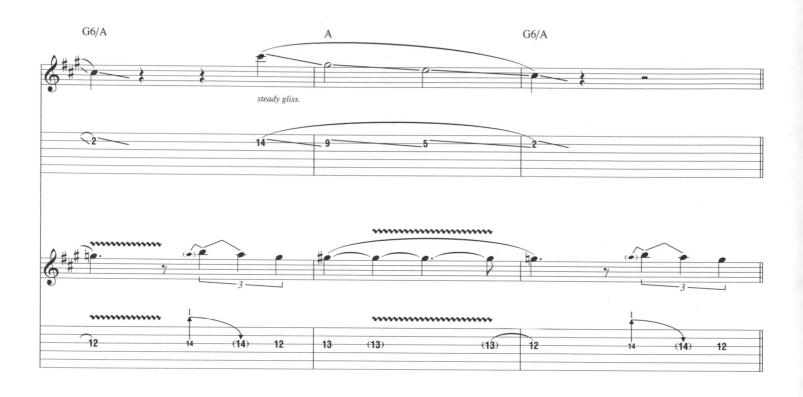

E

Gtr. 1: w/ Rhy. Fig. 1 (1st 9 meas.)
Gtr. 3: w/ Riff A

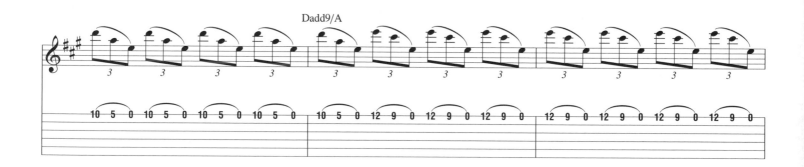

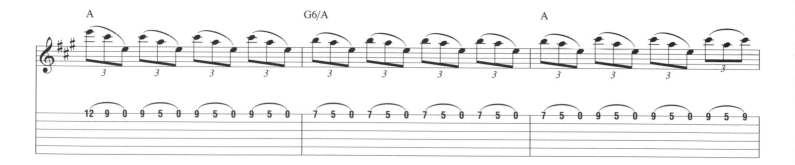

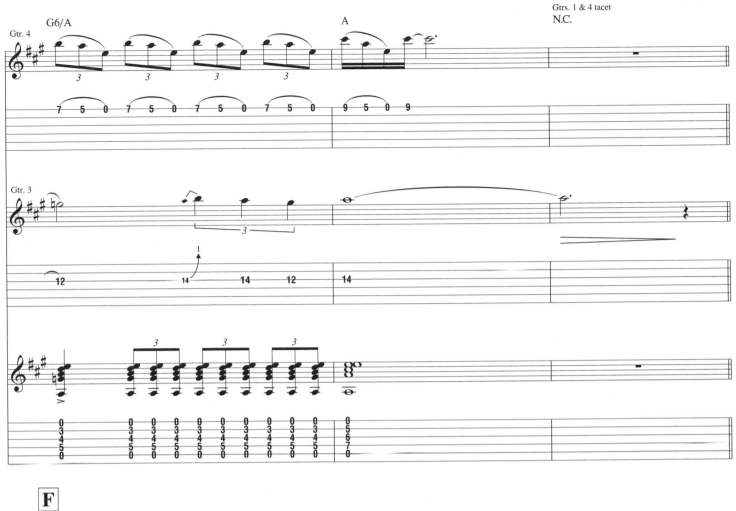

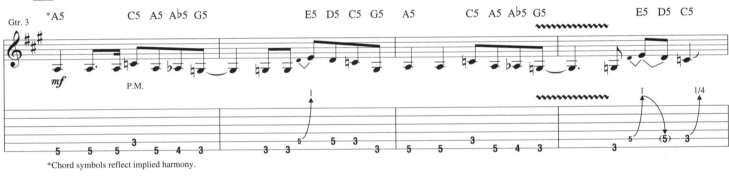

*Chord symbols reflect implied harmony.

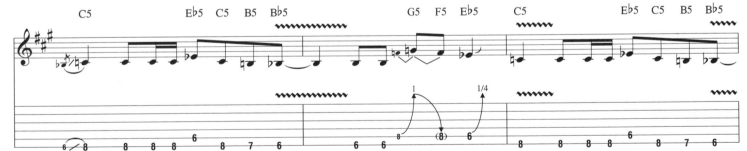

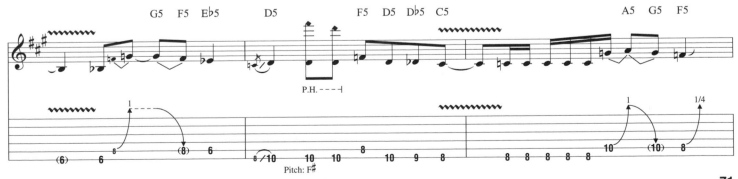

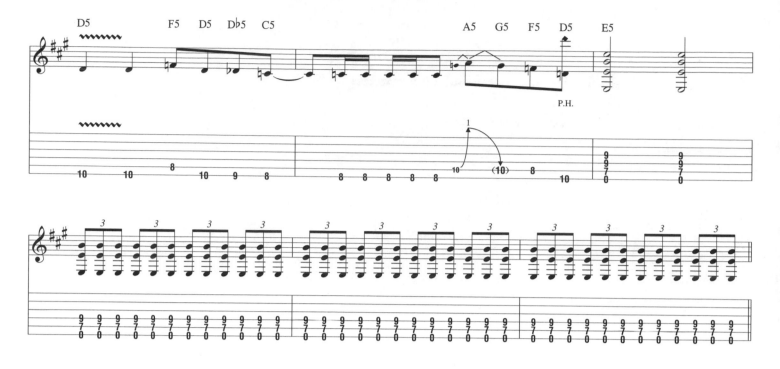

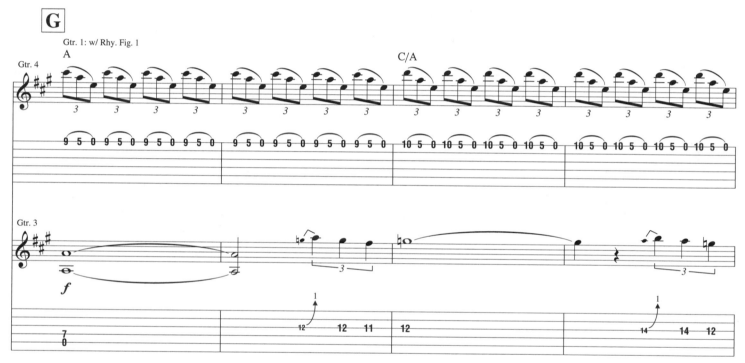

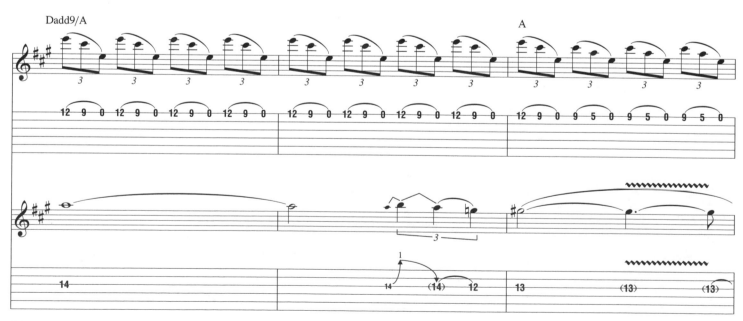

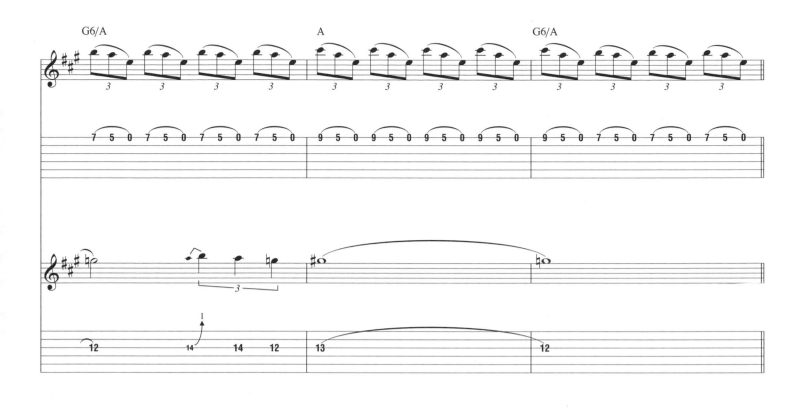

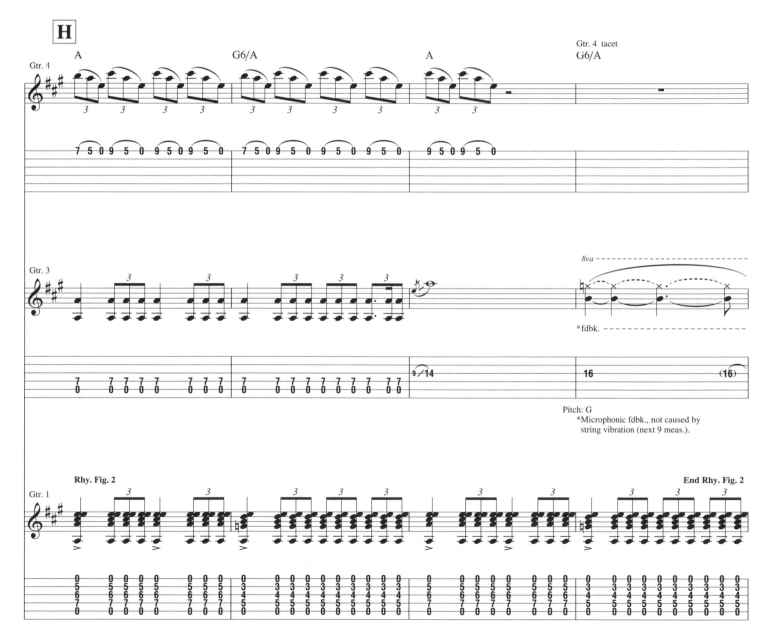

Blues Deluxe

Words and Music by Rod Stewart and Jeff Beck

*Set vol. knob at 1/2 volume.
**Recording sounds 1/4 step flat.
***Chord symbols reflect basic harmony.

Verse

2. I sit here in my lone - ly room, _____ tears _____ flow - in'

†Sung behind the beat.

all down my eyes. _____ C' - mon babe.

As I sit here, sit here, sit here in my lone - ly room, ah,

you know the tears flow - in' all _____ down my God darn eyes. _____

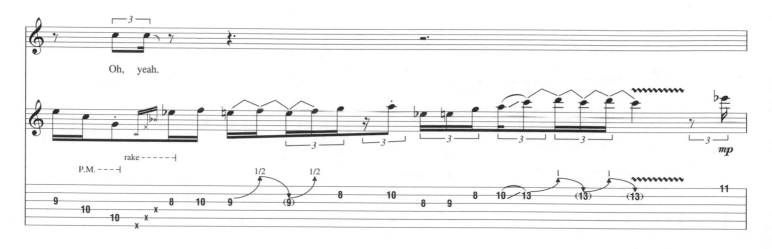

Oh, yeah.

G7   F7

I won- der how you could treat me so low - down and dir - ty.   Ha, ha.   You know what?   Your heart

C7   F7   C7   G7

must be made out of i - ron.   And it ain't no lie.   C'- mon ba - by.

Piano Solo

C7   F7   C7

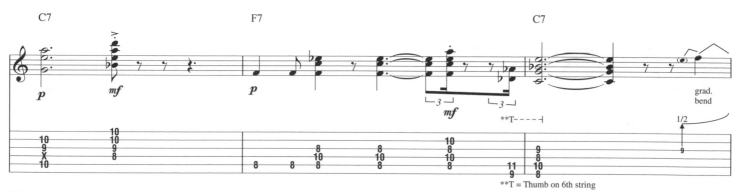

**T = Thumb on 6th string

78

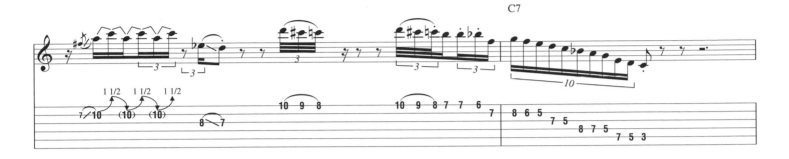

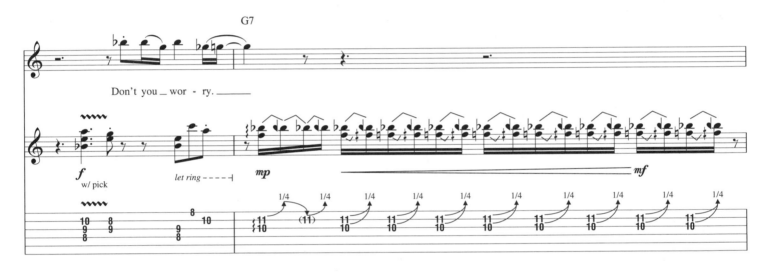

Don't you _ wor - ry. ____

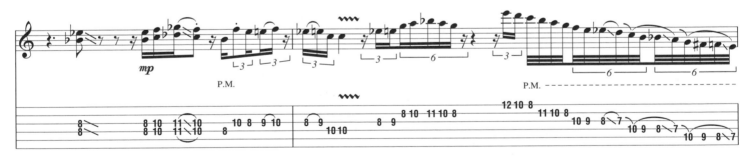

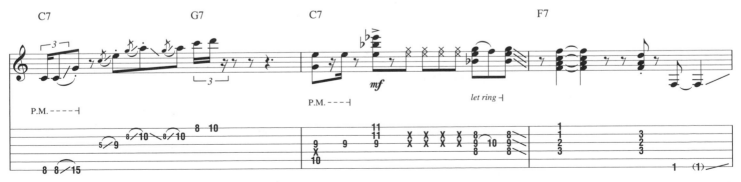

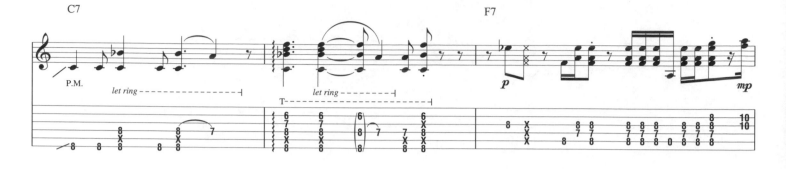

†Played ahead of the beat.   ††Sung behind the beat.

Guitar Solo

*Full vol.

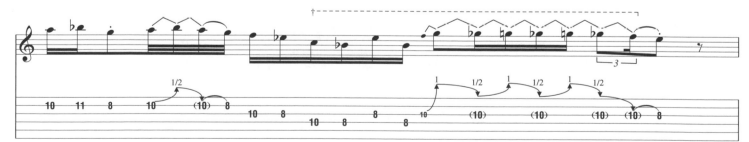

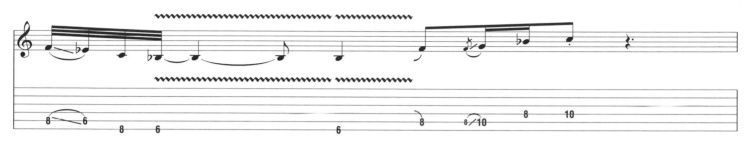

F7

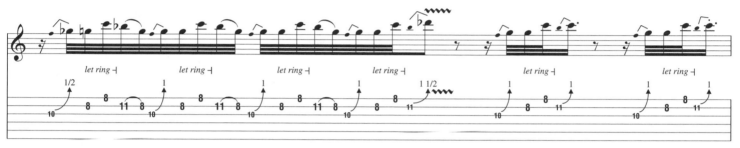

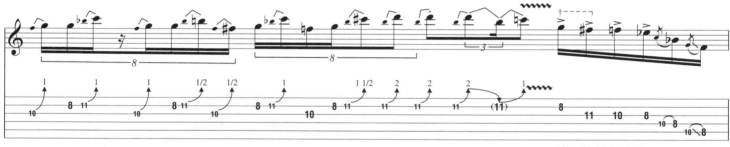

†Played behind the beat.

C7

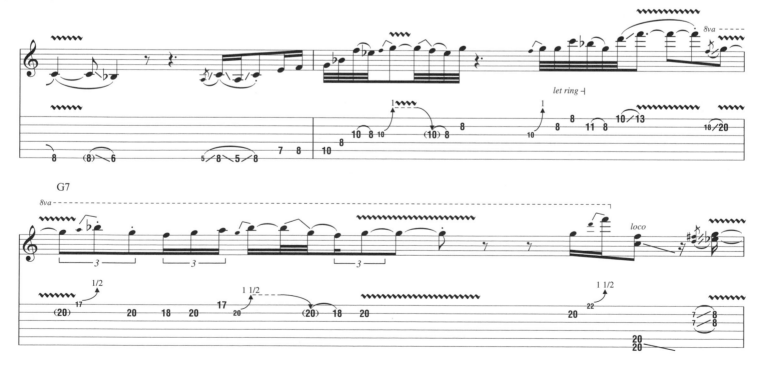

G7

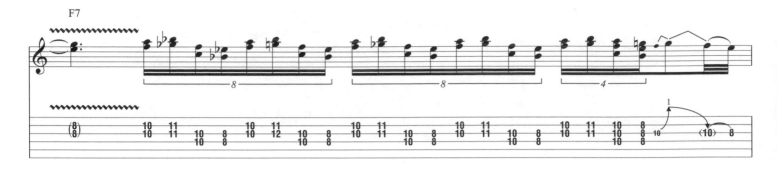

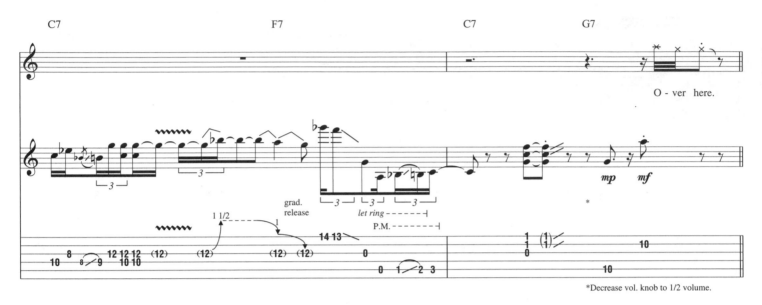

*Decrease vol. knob to 1/2 volume.

Verse

3. Some - time ___   I get so ___ wor - ried,   you   know ___

___   I could sit down   and cry.   Ha, ha, ha.   Yeah, I do.   Dig this.

F7

You know some-time I get so wor - - - ried,

mp

mf

peo - ple,

you know,—— and on - ly you know

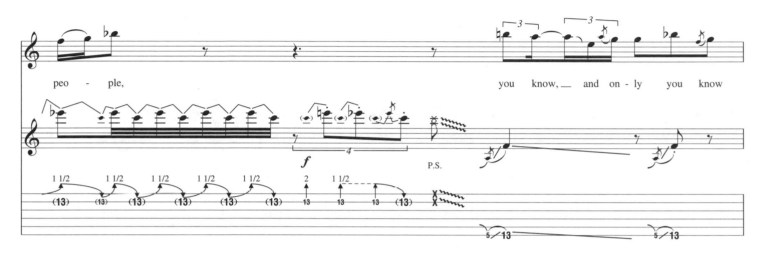

f

P.S.

C7

I could sit down and cry.———

And it ain't no lie.

Be - cause,

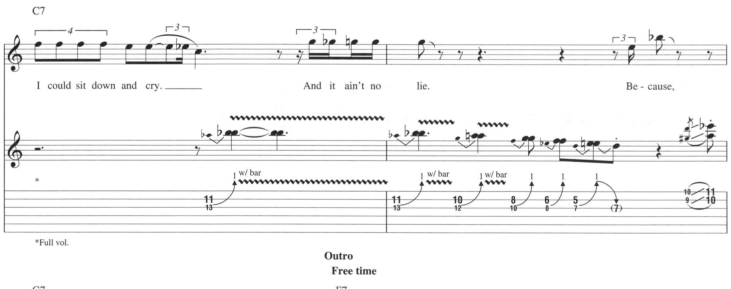

*Full vol.

Outro
Free time

G7

F7

I don't know too much a - bout love, peo - ple,

but I,————

**Decrease vol. knob to 1/4 volume.
***Vol. swell

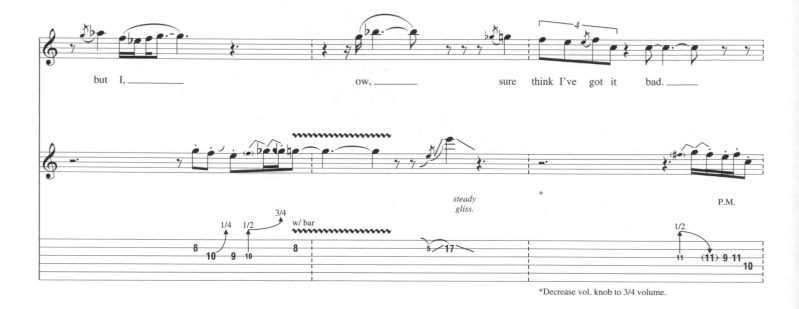

but I, _____ ow, _____ sure think I've got it bad. _____

*Decrease vol. knob to 3/4 volume.

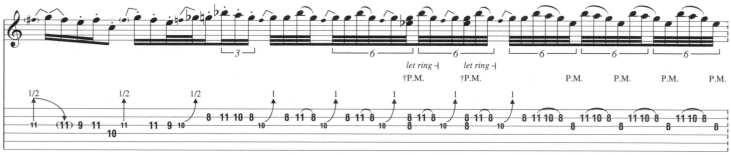

†P.M. 3rd string only.

Db7

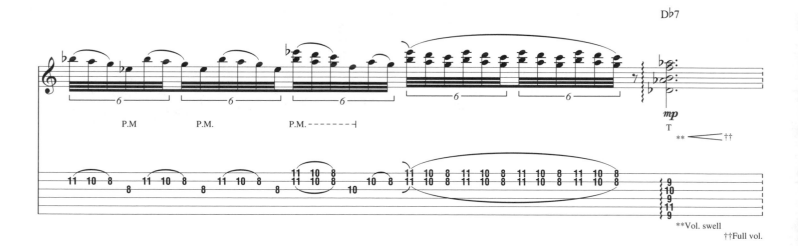

**Vol. swell
††Full vol.

C7

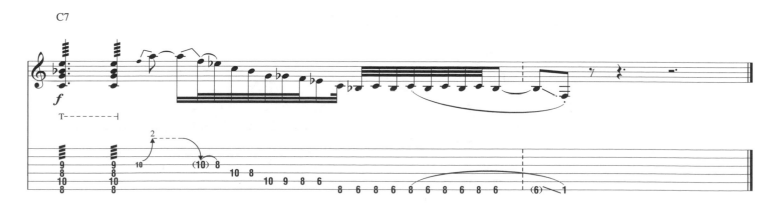

I Ain't Superstitious

Written by Willie Dixon

black cat crossed my __ trail. __   I ain't __ su-per-sti - tious,

but a black cat crossed my trail. __   Bad luck __ ain't got me so __ far,

*Sung as even eight notes.

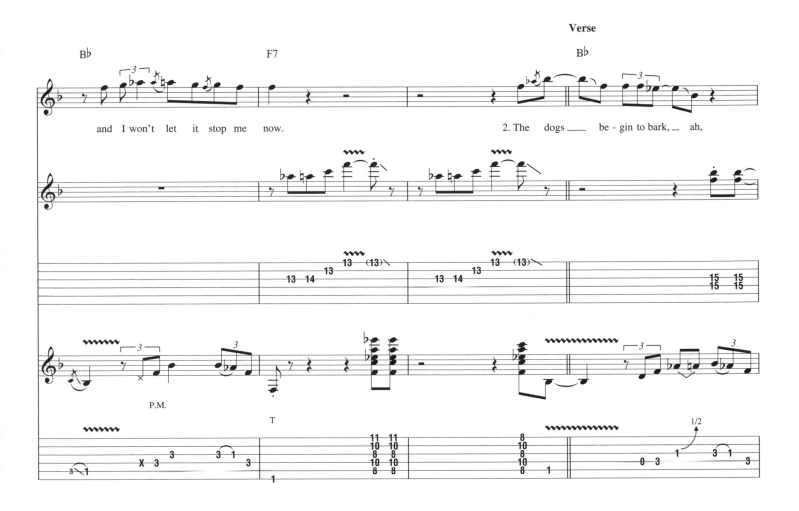

and I won't let it stop me now.

2. The dogs ___ be - gin to bark, ___ ah,

all o - ver my neigh - bor - hood, ___ and that ain't all.

Dogs ___ be - gin to bark, ___ ah,

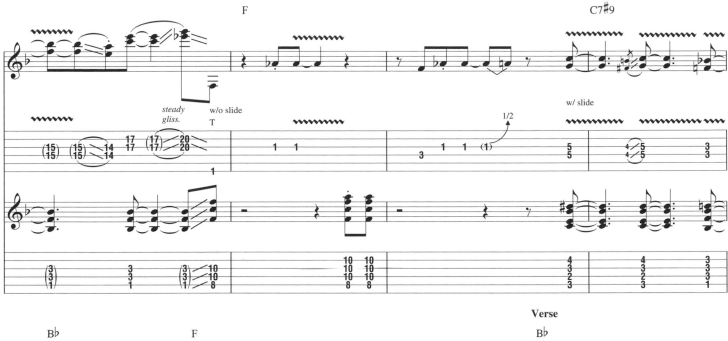

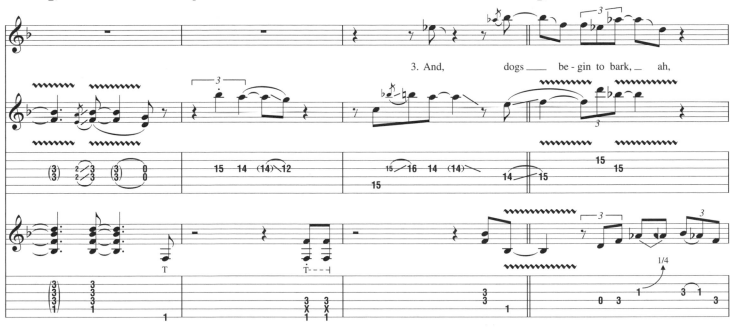

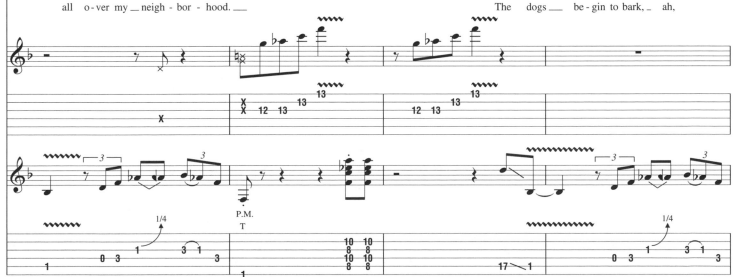

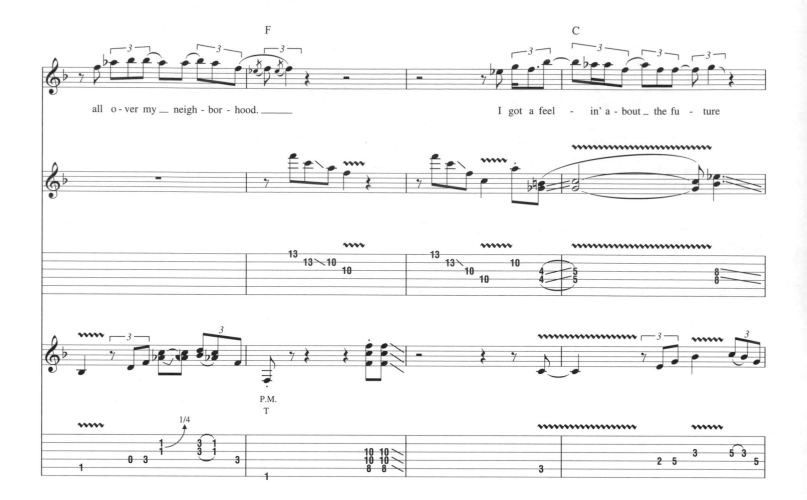

all o-ver my __ neigh-bor-hood. _____   I got a feel - in' a-bout __ the fu - ture

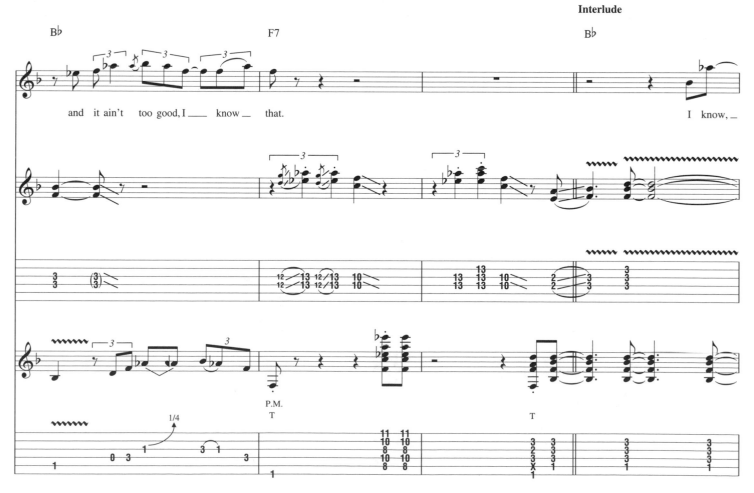

and it ain't too good, I __ know __ that.   I know, __

Interlude

but a black cat crossed my   trail, __   I said so man-y time be-fore.   Ain't __ su-per-sti - tious,

w/ slide

a black __ cat crossed my   trail, ah.   Bad   luck ain't got me so __ far

*Sung as even eight notes.

Outro

and you know I ain't gon - na let it stop me now.　　　　　　C' - mon.

*Back vol. down 1/2 way.

**Full vol.

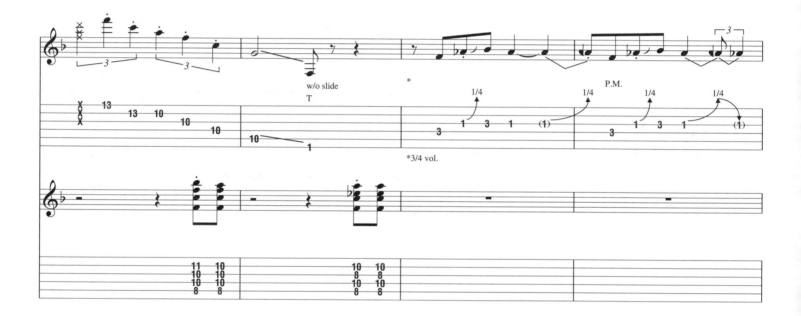

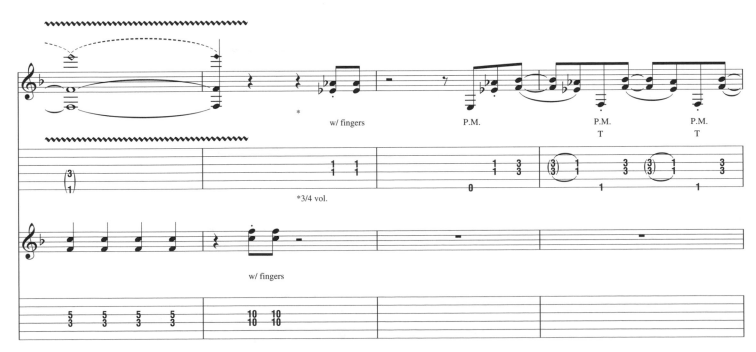

Free time

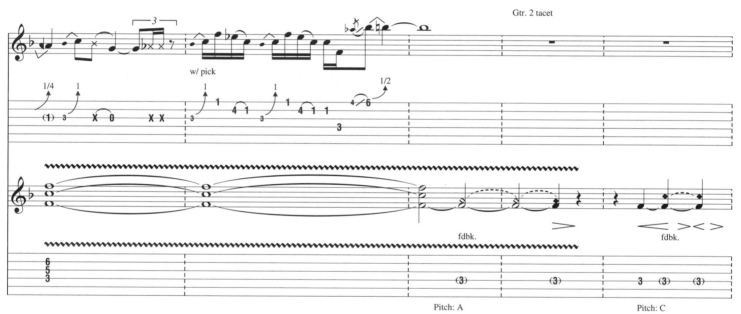

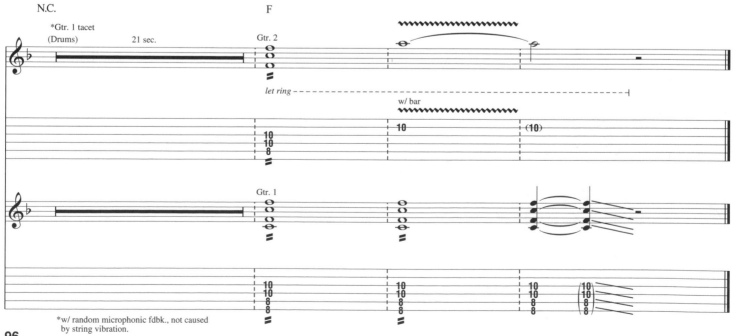

*w/ random microphonic fdbk., not caused
  by string vibration.